Emilie du Châtelet

Reflections on Happiness

Edited and translated by Sheila Oakley

ISBN: 9781520299686

CONTENTS

Preface

The subject of happiness and its attainment has, of course, been addressed by philosophers much further back in time than Madame du Châtelet. One thinks of the Ancient Greek philosophers, Plato and Aristotle, and of course the Epicureans and the Stoics had their own views on the subject. Religious texts and preachers of all faiths also offer many and varied opinions and explanations on how happiness, including the highest states of self-realization, fulfilment, or peace, may be attained. Even this perfunctory journey into the distant past, traversing centuries and continents, begins to reveal that the word 'happiness' is a very vague one. Attempts to define it by reference to other words in the same semantic field may offer us a deeper understanding, except that the simple abstract noun 'happiness' seems to send out sparks in many different directions. We might in the manner of the crossword addict think of 'contentment', 'joy', 'pleasure', 'satisfaction', 'bliss', 'serenity', 'fulfilment', 'ecstasy', 'euphoria' etc., and it also soon becomes apparent that there are states of happiness that are of comparatively short duration and others that have a longer time span.

What, then, does Madame du Châtelet have to say about happiness that has not been said by others before her or since, and that is therefore fresh, original, and inspiring? First of all, it should be said that she did not write this essay either for publication or for self-glory. On the contrary, it was not published until 1779, by which time she had been dead for almost thirty years. Even so, both the tone of her writing and the advice that she gives to the younger and less experienced reader (perhaps a mirror-image of her younger self) suggests that she hoped it would later be read by others and that posterity would recognize her as a woman of letters, as well as for her contribution to mathematics and science.

A great merit of this short essay is that Madame du Châtelet was not writing about happiness in a very detached and aloof frame of mind in a world far removed from the rest of humankind. While it is true that she was both well-to-do and comparatively privileged, she knew that her material comforts and indulgences would not save her from the miseries that threaten and plague other human beings, such as illness, the damaging effects of time, rejection in love, public humiliation or disapprobation, and the fear and inevitability of death.

Perhaps because she was writing as a form of catharsis rather than for notoriety, she addresses all of these subjects very directly and honestly, revealing her own human failings for all to see. Ironically, her essay on happiness was written by a woman who was deeply unhappy, almost to the point of contemplating suicide.

The short work seems to be part of the process by which she endeavours to pull herself out of her state of despair and heightened fragility. At the time of writing, her intimate relationship with Voltaire, whose life and company she had shared for over ten years, was coming to an end. She was bereft but, as she makes clear, not without sufficient mental resource to survive this blow to her heart, her vanity, and her self-respect. In this regard, she might serve as an example and an inspiration to others, both women and men, who abruptly experience the shock and grief of losing someone who was very important and precious to them, whether through rejection, abandonment, or the separation occasioned by certain illnesses or death.

What Madame du Châtelet has to say about happiness, the rational and analytical approach that she adopts, and her unashamed sensuality, should be of interest to modern readers of both sexes and all ages. Writing as she was in 1746, she laments the very limited opportunities for happiness through achievement and public recognition available to women at that time. Her own life was a testimony to these constraints, though she managed to exercise far more independence in forging her own destiny than most women of her time.

Her achievements were also quite exceptional. She translated works by the German philosopher, Leibnitz, into French as well as Sir Isaac Newton's major scientific work, *Principia Mathematica*, from Latin into French. At the age of thirty-two, she submitted an essay on the nature of fire to a competition held by the French Royal Academy of Sciences. She sent it in anonymously, having written it secretly in the evenings unbeknown to her soul mate and companion, Voltaire. He also submitted an essay, using his own name. Though neither of them won a prize, their contributions were later published by the Academy of Sciences. Madame du Châtelet thus became the first woman in France to have a scientific work published by this prestigious authority.

Nevertheless, she was better known among her contemporaries as the mistress of Voltaire; and just before her death after childbirth at the age of forty-three, as the woman who scandalized polite society by taking a lover twelve years younger than herself, and becoming pregnant by him. She was fully aware that the social and moral rules that applied to women were quite different from those applied to men. For this reason, some of her advice on happiness is specifically directed towards women as opposed to both sexes.

It may be interesting to evaluate the extent to which the condition of women in the 21st century has progressed since she wrote this essay. In many respects, the situation of modern women is radically different from that of Madame du Châtelet, but perhaps in certain other respects, the traditional obstacles, prejudices, social stereotypes, and cultural constraints still endure. On the subject of time passing, Madame du Châtelet is not very charitable, either towards herself or to other women. While she talks about the great advantages of wisdom and experience, at times she seems to make no distinction between maturity, old age, and decrepitude, as far as women are concerned.

Her profound pessimism with regard to women in their prime clearly reflects her particular mental state at the time of writing, but also seems to perpetuate a vision of woman constructed by society, and by traditional attitudes and judgements regarding women's purpose and their value. It is a perspective on women that dates back over centuries and even millennia, and shows little sign of being cast aside.

In translating this essay from the French, I have endeavoured to remain faithful to the original work, while also adopting a style that is fluent and easy to read in English. There are many occasions when Madame du Châtelet uses the term 'One' as in 'One ought to...', and I have sometimes preferred to translate this as 'we', mainly because 'one' sounds more pompous and condescending in English than in French, where it is commonplace; but also because I wanted to replicate the writer's open, conversational tone of complicity with the reader.

I have also omitted one short passage which, though historically of great interest, is not of direct relevance to her central theme and would probably offend many readers, as it does myself. Since the aim of the book is to offer the reader advice on how to attain happiness, rather than to hurt sensibilities, the passage has been omitted. The astute reader will appreciate that any work of literature or art should be understood both in relation to when it was written, and the universal significance and meaning that it may contain. Madame du Châtelet was both a very original and independent thinker and a product of her time, and she sometimes displays an insensitivity towards those affected by illness or disability that was common in the 18th century but which would shock most modern readers.

I have also introduced sub-headings and made some changes to punctuation and paragraph lengths, purely with the purpose of facilitating reading. In translating this work, I have endeavoured to accurately convey the original meaning, and replicate the style and tone of its writer, a woman who was charming, amusing, extraordinary, outstanding, and irrepressible.

Sheila Oakley

Please note: An * after certain names and words in the text invites the reader to consult the Notes on the Text beginning at page 29. The notes on the text may be read either simultaneously with Emilie du Châtelet's essay, or consulted afterwards during a second reading. This latter option may be more enjoyable for the reader, and it is an essay that merits the trouble of being read at least twice.

Reflections on Happiness – Emilie du Châtelet

Initial reflections

It is commonly believed that happiness is difficult to achieve, and there is every reason to think this; but among men and women it would be easier to attain if reflection and forethought preceded their actions. We are dragged along by circumstances and give ourselves up to hopes that are never more than half-fulfilled. Moreover, we clearly perceive the means to be happy only when age and the impediments that we have created place obstacles in the way.

Let us consider these reflections that arise too late: those who read this will find here what age and the circumstances of their life will furnish too slowly. Let us prevent them from losing a portion of the brief and precious time that they have to feel and to think in making their vessel impermeable when they should be seeking out the pleasures that may be enjoyed during the navigation.

To be happy we need to strip away our prejudices, be virtuous, enjoy good health, have tastes and passions, be susceptible to illusions, since we owe the majority of our pleasures to illusion, and unhappy is the person who loses that capacity. Far from seeking therefore to make it disappear by the torch of reason, let us try to thicken the veneer that it places upon the majority of objects. Illusion is even more necessary to them than are care and adornments to our bodies.

We must begin by clearly telling and convincing ourselves that we have nothing to do in this world than to obtain for ourselves agreeable sensations and sentiments. The moralists who say to us, 'repress your passions and master your desires if you want to be happy', do not know the path to happiness. We are happy only through satisfied tastes and passions; I say tastes because one is not always sufficiently happy to be able to have passions, and in the absence of passions, we have to be content with tastes. It is therefore passions that we should ask of God, if we dare ask him for something; and Le Nôtre* was perfectly right to ask the Pope for temptations instead of indulgences.

But, you may say to me, surely the passions produce more unhappy people than happy ones? I don't have the set of scales needed to weigh the good and bad they have generally caused mankind; but it should be noted that unhappy people are known about because they need others. They like to recount their woes, and they seek remedies and relief. Happy people seek nothing and are not going to alert others to their happiness. The unhappy are interesting, the happy are unknown.

This is why, when two lovers are reconciled, when their jealousy is at an end, when the obstacles that separated them are overcome, they are no longer a fitting subject for theatre. The drama is over for the audience. The scenario between Renaud and Armide* would not interest us as much as it does if the audience were not already aware that Renaud's love is the result of an enchantment that will be dispelled, and that the passion that Armide displays in this scene makes her unhappiness more interesting. The forces that act upon our soul to move it during theatrical performances and in life's events are the same. We are therefore much more familiar with love by the miseries that it causes than by the happiness, often obscure, that it spreads through people's lives.

But let's suppose for a moment that the passions produce a greater number of unhappy people than happy ones. I say that they would still be desirable, because it is the condition without which we cannot experience great pleasures. Now life is only worth living in order to have pleasant sensations and feelings; and the more intense the agreeable feelings, the happier one is. It is therefore desirable to be susceptible to passions, and I will repeat: it is a shame for the person who isn't.

It is up to us to make passions serve our happiness, and that often depends upon ourselves. Whoever has known how to make the most of their situation and of the circumstances in which life has placed them, and whoever has managed to achieve peace of mind, and be receptive to all the feelings and the agreeable sensations that this condition can provide is assuredly an excellent philosopher, and ought to truly thank nature. I speak of their condition and the circumstances in which destiny has placed them, because I think that one of the things that contributes the most to happiness is to be content with our situation, and to dream rather of making it happy than of changing it.

My purpose is not to write for all kinds of conditions and all kinds of people; not all situations are conducive to the same kind of happiness. I write only for those who might be called people of the world, that is to say, for those who are born with a ready-made fortune, more or less brilliant, more or less opulent, but lastly such that they can remain in their situation without embarrassment, and these are perhaps not the easiest people to make happy.

Good health

But to have passions, to be able to satisfy them, it is undoubtedly necessary to enjoy good health; that is first and foremost. Now, this benefit is not as independent of ourselves as we might think. As we are all born healthy (I say, in general) and made to last a certain time, it is certain that if we don't destroy our constitution by greed, habitual late nights, or various excesses, we would all live more or less to what is called the age of man. Here I exclude violent deaths that one cannot foresee and which it is therefore pointless to dwell upon.

But, you may retort, if your passion is gourmandise, you will therefore be very unhappy since if you want to be in good health, you should perpetually restrain yourself. To that I reply that, happiness being your goal, in satisfying your passions nothing must lead you astray from this goal; and if the stomach-ache or gout that you give yourself by overindulgence causes you pains that are more intense than the pleasure you derive from satisfying your appetite, you miscalculate in preferring the delight in one to the avoidance of the other. You lose sight of your goal and you are unhappy through your own fault.

Do not complain that you are a gourmand, since this passion is a source of continual pleasure, but know how to make it serve your happiness. That will be easy for you if you stay at home, and if you have served what you want to eat. Go on periodic diets. If you wait until your stomach experiences a real hunger, everything offered to you will give you as much pleasure as more refined dishes, which you will not dream of when they are not before your eyes. This sobriety that you will have imposed upon yourself will make the pleasure keener. I don't recommend it in order to extinguish the gourmand in you, but to prepare you for a more exquisite delight.

Once we are firmly persuaded that without health we cannot enjoy any pleasure or any good, we resolve without difficulty to make a few sacrifices to conserve our own health. I am, I can admit, an example of this. I have a very good constitution, but I am not at all robust, and there are things that would certainly destroy my health. Wine is one such example, as well as all the liqueurs; I have refrained from them since my youth. I have the sort of constitution that is badly affected by alcohol for the entire morning after.

Moreover, I indulge too often in the gourmandise with which God has endowed me, and I compensate for these excesses by undertaking a strict diet the moment I feel the negative effect, and this has always enabled me to avoid illnesses. These diets cost me nothing. At these times I always stay at home during meal times and since nature is wise enough not to give us hunger pangs when we have overindulged ourselves with food, my appetite not being stimulated by the presences of dishes, I deny myself nothing in not eating, and I restore my health without any deprivation.

Freedom from prejudices

Another source of happiness is to be free from prejudices, and it is only *we* who can rid ourselves of them. We all have the mental capacity to examine the things that are presented to us as true; to know, for example if two and two make four, or five. Moreover, in this century, there's no shortage of help for educating ourselves. I know that there are other prejudices than those of religion, and I think it's good to shake them up. Even so, there is none that has such an influence upon our happiness and our unhappiness as that of religion. By prejudice I mean an opinion that we have accepted without examination, because it wouldn't stand up to it. Error can never be a good thing, and it is certainly a great harm in matters upon which the conduct of our lives depend.

We mustn't confuse prejudices with good manners. Prejudices contain no truth, and can be of no use except to malicious souls, for there are depraved souls just as there are deformed bodies. The former are beyond the pale and I have nothing to say to them. Good manners have a truth by convention, and that is sufficient that every well-intentioned person never allows him or herself to cast them aside. There is no book that teaches good manners, and yet nobody ignores them in good faith. They vary according to conditions, generations, and circumstances. Whoever strives for happiness must never brush them aside.

The correct observance of good manners is a virtue, and I have said that to be happy we must be virtuous. I know that the preachers, and even Juvenal*, say that we should love virtue for itself, for its own beauty, but we need to understand the sense of these words, and we will see that they amount to this: we must be virtuous, because we cannot be malicious and happy. I understand by *vertu** everything that contributes to the happiness of society and as a consequence our own, since we are members of society.

I say that one cannot be happy and vicious, and the demonstration of this axiom may be found in the depths of every person's heart. I maintain, even to the worst scoundrels, that there are none for whom the pangs of conscience, that is to say of their inner feelings, and the contempt which they feel they merit and which they experience when exposed, does not serve as a punishment. By scoundrels, I do not mean thieves, murderers, or poisoners.

These cannot be found among the class of those for whom I write; rather, I give this name to false and treacherous people, to slanderers, denouncers, ungrateful people, in short to all those tainted by vices against which there are no laws, but against which the moral codes of society have brought judgements all the more terrible for always being exercised. I maintain therefore that there is nobody on earth who can feel that they are despised without despairing. This public contempt, this disapprobation by good people, is a crueller punishment than all those that a court judge could inflict, because it lasts longer and is never accompanied by hope.

We should therefore not be malevolent if we do not want to be unhappy; but it is not enough for us *not* to be unhappy. Life would not be worth the trouble of being endured if the absence of pain was our only goal. Nothingness would be preferable: for assuredly it is the state in which one suffers the least. One must therefore attempt to be happy. We need to be content with ourselves for the same reason that we need to be comfortably lodged in our homes, and it would be foolish to hope for this satisfaction without virtue.

One easily dazzles the eyes of mortals, but one cannot deceive the watchful eye of the gods*,

So said one of our best poets; but it is the vigilant eye of our own conscience that is never deceived.

We give ourselves a just assessment, and the more we can honestly claim that we have fulfilled our duties, that we have done all the good that we could have done, in short that we are virtuous, the more we taste this inner satisfaction that may be called the health of the soul. I doubt if there is a more delightful feeling than that which one experiences when one has just done a good deed, which deserves the esteem of sincere people. To the inner pleasure occasioned by good deeds is further added the pleasure of enjoying universal esteem: for rogues cannot deny the worth of integrity, but the esteem of honest people is the only merit worthy of consideration.

Susceptibility to illusions

Lastly, I say that to be happy, we need to be susceptible to illusion, and that hardly needs proving; but, you will say to me, I have said that error is always harmful: isn't illusion an error? No. As a matter of fact, illusion does not make us see objects exactly as they ought to be so as to give us agreeable sensations, it adapts them to our nature. Such are optical illusions: now the eye does not deceive us, even though it doesn't make us see the objects as they are. It makes us see them in a way that we need to see them for our utility. Why do I laugh more than anybody at puppets, if it isn't because I lend myself more than anybody else to illusion, and after a quarter of an hour believe that it is Polichinelle* speaking?

Would we have a moment's pleasure at the theatre, if we did not submit to the illusion that makes us see people we know to be long since dead, and makes them speak in alexandrine verse*? But what pleasure would we have during another performance where everything is illusion, if we didn't know how to suspend disbelief? Assuredly, we would lose a lot. Those who, at the opera, derive enjoyment only from the music and the dancing, experience there a pleasure greatly diminished and below that offered by the entirety of such an enchanting performance. I give the example of stage performances because the illusion here is easy to discern.

Illusion blends with all the pleasures of our life, and it provides the varnish. You will perhaps say that this does not depend upon us, and that is only too true, up to a certain point. We cannot give ourselves illusions, just as we cannot give ourselves tastes or passions; but we can preserve the illusions that we have. We can refrain from destroying them; we can avoid going behind the scenes to see the wheels that make the flights, and the other machines: this is all the artistry that is employed, and this artistry is neither useless nor fruitless.

These are the great driving forces of happiness, if I can express myself thus; but there remain many fine points of detail that can contribute to our happiness.

A clear sense of purpose

The most fundamental thing of all is to be clearly decided about what one wants to be and what one wants to do, and this is what almost all people lack. It is however the condition without which there is no happiness. Without it, we swim perpetually in a sea of uncertainties; we destroy in the morning what we have made the evening before. We pass our life in making foolish errors, in putting them right, in regretting them.

This feeling of regret is one of the most pointless and the most unpleasant that our soul can experience. One of the great secrets is to know how to guard against it. As nothing in life ever replicates itself exactly, it is almost always pointless to examine our faults, or at least to dwell upon them for a long time, to scrutinize them, and to reproach ourselves for them. This is to cover ourselves in confusion in our own eyes to no advantage. We must depart from where we are, employ all the wisdom we possess to correct faults and to find the means to make good; but we should *not* keep looking back with regret, and we must always cast from our minds the memory of our mistakes. Once we have grasped the lessons to be drawn, casting aside sad thoughts and substituting them with pleasant ones is also one of the great springs of happiness, and we have that within our power, at least up to a certain point.

I know that in a violent passion that makes us unhappy, it is not entirely within our control to banish from our mind the ideas that afflict us; but we are not always in these extreme situations. Not all illnesses are malignant fevers; and petty, irksome troubles, or unpleasant feelings, however mild, are best avoided. Death, for example, is an idea that always troubles us, either when we foresee our own, or when we think of that of the people we love. We must therefore carefully avoid everything that can remind us of this idea.

I strongly disagree with Montaigne*, who congratulated himself on being so accustomed to death that he was sure that he would be able to stare it in the face without being afraid. We see, by the complacency with which he recounts this victory that it cost him a great deal, and in this the wise Montaigne had miscalculated. For assuredly it is a folly to poison the short time that we have to live by this sad and humiliating idea, in order to bear more patiently a moment that bodily suffering always makes very bitter, whatever our philosophy. Furthermore, who knows if the enfeebling of our mind, caused by illness or age, will allow us to gather the fruit of our reflections, or if we will be caught unawares, as is so often the case in this life?

Let us always bear in mind, whenever we think of death, this line by Gresset *:

Pain is a century, and death a moment

Let's cast the mind aside from all disagreeable ideas; they are the source of all metaphysical ills, and it is almost always those, above all, that we have the power to avoid.

Wisdom and the love of study

Wisdom must always lead in the game: for being wise is synonymous with being happy, at least in my dictionary. One needs to have passions to be happy but they must be made to serve our happiness, and there are some that must be denied entry into our soul. I'm not referring here to passions that are vices, such as hatred, vengeance, or anger. However, ambition, for example, is a passion against which we need to protect our soul, if we want to be happy. It's not through the absence of reason that it brings no enjoyment, since I think this passion can provide it. It is not because ambition is always desirous, for that's certainly a great good, but it is because, of all the passions, it is the one that makes our happiness dependent on others.

Now, the less our happiness depends on others, the more it is easy for us to be happy. Let's not be afraid of being too inflexible on this point, it will always depend quite enough on others. By virtue of its independent nature, the love of study is, of all the passions, the one that contributes most to our happiness. In the love of study is contained a passion from which an elevated soul is never entirely exempt, that of glory. Indeed, for half the world there is even *only* this means of experiencing this passion, and it is precisely from this half that upbringing removes the means, and renders the taste for it impossible.

It is unquestionable that the love of study is much less necessary to men's happiness than to women's. Men have an infinite range of means to be happy that are entirely lacking for women. They have many other means of achieving glory, and it is certain that the ambition to render these talents useful to their country and serve their fellow citizens, either by their capability in the art of war, or by their talents in government, or business affairs greatly exceeds what study can offer.

Women are excluded, by their condition, from every kind of glory, and when, by chance, it happens that a woman is born with a sufficiently elevated soul, study is all that remains to console her for all the excluded domains and all the forms of dependency to which she finds herself condemned by virtue of her condition.

The love of glory, which is the source of so much pleasure and so much effort of all kinds that contribute to the happiness, education, and perfection of society, is entirely based on illusion. Nothing is easier than to exorcize the ghost after which all elevated souls run, but just think of what they and others would lose! I know that there is a certain solidity in the love of glory that one can relish while alive; but there are hardly any heroes, in whatever domain, who want to entirely disregard the recognition of posterity, from which we expect even greater justice than from our contemporaries. We don't ceaselessly relish the vague desire to be talked about when we are no longer alive; but it always remains in the depths of our heart. Philosophy would like to present it as vanity; but this feeling carries us away, and its pleasure is in no way an illusion: for it demonstrates to us the great worth in taking delight in our future reputation.

If the present were our only boon, our pleasures would be considerably more limited than they are. We are happy at the present moment, not only because of our enjoyment now, but through our hopes, through our reminiscences. The present is enriched by the past and the future. Who would work for their children, for the grandeur of their house, if they did not take pleasure in the future? We are right to do so: self-love is always the more or less hidden motive of our actions; it is the wind that swells the sails, without which the vessel wouldn't move.

I said that the love of study was the passion most necessary to our happiness; it is a reliable resource against misfortunes, and a well of inexhaustible pleasure. Cicero* is quite right to say:

The pleasures of the senses and those of the heart are, undoubtedly, above those of study; it is not necessary to study to be happy; but it is perhaps necessary to feel that one always has this resource and this support.

We can enjoy study and spend entire years, perhaps our life, without studying; and happy are those who spend it thus: for it can only be to more intense pleasures that they sacrifice a pleasure that they are always sure to find, and that they will make sufficiently exciting to compensate them for the loss of the others.

Being content with our lot

One of the great secrets of happiness is to modify our desires and to love the things that we possess. Nature, the aim of which is always our happiness, (and I understand by nature all that is instinct and without reason), nature, I say, gives us desires only in conformity with our condition. We desire only by degrees: an infantry captain desires to be a colonel, and he is in no way unhappy that he is not commanding armies, whatever talent he feels that he has. It is up to our mind and our reflections to reinforce this wise sobriety of nature. We are happy only through satisfied desires; we ought thus to allow ourselves to desire only those things that can be obtained without too much trouble or work, and it is a way in which we can do a great deal for our happiness.

To love what we possess, to know how to delight in it, to savour the advantages of our situation, not to preoccupy ourselves too much with those who seem to us to be happier, to strive to perfect our own lot and to derive the maximum from it, this is what we ought to call happiness; and I think I provide a good definition when I say that the happiest of human beings are those who least desire a change in their condition. To delight in this happiness, one needs to cure or prevent a sickness of another kind that is entirely at odds with it and that is only too common. It is anxiety. This mental disposition militates against all enjoyment, and in consequence every kind of happiness.

The wise philosophy or, in other words, the firm persuasion that we have nothing else to do in this world than to be happy, is a certain remedy against this affliction, which rarely affects wise souls capable of embracing principles and their implications.

There is a passion which is very foolish in the eyes of philosophers and reason, the motive for which, however it is disguised, is even humiliating and should alone suffice to cure it, but which can even so induce happiness: it is the passion for gambling*. It is a pleasure to indulge in it, if we can moderate it and reserve it for the time in our life when this resource will be necessary for us, and this time is old age. The love of gambling is undoubtedly rooted in the love of money. It is not at all odd that a large bet (and by large bet I mean that which can make a difference to our circumstances) has a certain appeal.

Our soul wants to be stirred by the hope or the fear; it is happy only through the things that make it feel its existence. Now gambling puts us perpetually on tenterhooks via these two passions and consequently holds our soul in an emotional state that is one of the great sources of happiness that exists within us. The pleasure that gambling has given me has often consoled me for not being rich. I believe that my temperament is such that a windfall, trivial for somebody else, is suffice to make me happy; and if that should befall me, gambling would become insipid to me. At least I feared it would, and this idea convinced me that I owed the pleasure in gambling to my modest means and used it to comfort myself.

There is no doubt that physical needs are the source of sensual pleasures, and I am convinced that there is more pleasure to be had from a modest fortune than from a great abundance. A box, a piece of porcelain, a new item of furniture, are a real joy for me; but if I had thirty boxes, I would hardly notice the thirty–first. Our tastes deaden easily when fully satisfied, and we ought to offer thanks to God for having given us the privations necessary to conserve them. This is why a king becomes bored so easily, and it is impossible for him to be happy, unless he has received from heaven a soul sufficiently large to be sensitive to the pleasures of his situation, that is to say, that of being able to make a great many people happy. Then, this condition surpasses all others in terms of both happiness and power.

Love, the supreme happiness

I have said that the more our happiness depends upon ourselves, the more it is assured; and yet the passion that can give us the greatest pleasure and the most happiness makes us entirely dependent upon others for them: you see, of course, that I want to speak of love.

This passion is perhaps the only one that can make us really desire to live, and inspire us to thank the author of nature, whatever that may be, for having given us existence. Mylord Rochester* was quite right to say that the gods had placed this heavenly drop in life's holy cup to give us the courage to bear it:

One must love; it is that which sustains us: for without love, it is sad to be human.

If this mutual desire, which is a sixth sense, and the finest, the most delicate, the most precious of all, chances to bring together two souls equally susceptible to happiness, to pleasure, all is said, there is nothing more to do to be happy, all the rest is indifferent; only good health is required. We must employ all the faculties of our soul in delighting in this happiness. Life seems quite pointless if we lose it, and you can be sure that all the years of Nestor* are worth nothing compared to a quarter of an hour of such joy.

It is true that such a happiness is rare. If it were common, it would be considerably better to be a human being than a god, at least in so far as we can imagine that. The best we can do is to persuade ourselves that this happiness is not impossible.

However, I don't know if love has ever brought together two people so made for each other that they never experience the satiety of joy, nor the cooling off that security brings, nor the indolence or the lukewarm feeling born of the ease and continuity of a relationship, in which the illusion remains intact (for where does illusion feature more than in love?), and finally, where the ardour is as strong in the fulfilment as in the deprivation, and can withstand misfortunes and pleasures equally. A heart capable of such a love, a soul so tender and so steadfast might seem to have exhausted the power of the divinity. There is only one born in a century; to produce two would seem to be beyond its force, or if it produced them, it would be jealous of their pleasures, should they meet each other.

Even so, love can make us happy at less expense: a tender and sensitive soul is happy in the single pleasure that it finds in loving. I don't mean by that that one can be perfectly happy in loving, even if one is not loved; but I am saying that, even though our ideas of happiness are not entirely fulfilled by the love of the person that we love, the pleasure that we feel in giving ourselves over to all our tenderness can be enough to make us happy; and if this soul still has the good fortune to be susceptible to illusion, it will certainly believe itself to be more loved than it perhaps really is. It must love so much, that it loves for two, and so that the warmth of the heart supplies that which is really lacking to its happiness.

Without doubt, a person of a sensitive, intense, and passionate predisposition must pay a price for all the drawbacks of such qualities, and I don't know whether to call them good or bad qualities; but I believe that anyone, of whatever temperament, can experience such heartache.

A first love can be so overwhelming to someone of this predisposition that the soul is incapable of all reflection and all moderate ideas; without doubt, it can be the prelude to great sorrows. But the greatest hardship attached to this passionate sensibility is that it is impossible that somebody who loves with such excess can be loved, and that there is hardly any man whose desire does not diminish by the experience of such a passion. That must undoubtedly seem very strange to anyone who does not yet know the human heart well enough; but though one may have reflected little upon what experience offers, it seems apparent that in order to retain a lover's heart for a long time, hope and fear must always act upon it.

Now, a passion such as I have just described leads to an abandonment of the self, making one incapable of all artfulness. Love penetrates from all sides; we begin by adoring the other person, it would be impossible otherwise; but before long the certainty of being loved, and the boredom of being always prisoner, the misfortune of having nothing to fear deadens the senses. This is how the human heart is made, and don't for a moment believe that I'm speaking from bitterness.

It is true that God bestowed upon me one of these tender and immutable souls which knows neither how to disguise nor how to moderate their passions, which knows neither loss of ardour nor distaste, and the tenacity of which withstands everything, even the certainty of no longer being loved; but I was happy for ten years through the love of someone who had subjugated my soul; and these ten years were spent in intimacy with him, without one moment of loathing, or of weariness.

Ebbing passion

When age, sickness, perhaps also to some degree the ease of pleasure, diminished passion's keenness, for a long time I was oblivious of this. I loved for two, I passed my entire life with him, and my heart, devoid of suspicion, delighted in the pleasure of loving and in the illusion of believing myself loved. It is true that I have lost this immensely happy state of mind, and this hasn't been without it costing me many tears. One needs a terrible jolt to break such chains: the gash in my heart bled for a long time; I had reason to pity myself and I forgave everything.

I was sufficiently fair to feel that there was perhaps in the world only my heart that had this immutability that annihilates the impact of time; that if age and ill health had not entirely extinguished desires, I might perhaps again experience them and love would return them to me; lastly, that his heart, incapable of love, felt for me the most tender friendship, and he might have devoted his life to me. The certainty that a rekindling of his desire and his passion was impossible, since I know full well that this is contrary to nature, led my heart imperceptibly to a peaceful feeling of friendship, and this feeling, joined with my passion for study, made me quite content.

But can such a tender heart be fulfilled by a sentiment as placid and as weak as that of friendship? I do not know if it is even desirable to keep trying to hold on to a sentiment akin to apathy when the heart recoils from it. We are happy only through intense and pleasant feelings; why then forbid ourselves the most intense and most agreeable of all? But what has been experienced, the inevitable reflections that have brought the heart to this apathy, even the trouble it has had in curbing its desire, must make one afraid to leave a condition that is not unhappy to endure woes that age and the loss of beauty make pointless.

The gift of experience

Very pleasant thoughts, you will tell me, and very useful! You will see how they will be of use to you, if ever you desire somebody who falls in love with you; but I think you are mistaken if you believe that these reflections are of no value. Beyond the age of thirty, the passions do not overwhelm us with the same impetuosity. You believe that you would resist your inclination if you really wanted to, and if you were convinced that it would lead to unhappiness. We succumb only because we are not convinced of the soundness of these maxims, and we hope once more to be happy, and we are right to persuade ourselves of it.

Why forbid ourselves the hope of being happy, and in the most intense way? But if we shouldn't deny ourselves this hope, we are not allowed to be mistaken regarding the means of happiness. Experience must at least teach us to reckon with ourselves, and to make our passions serve our happiness. We can take things upon ourselves up to a certain point; we cannot do everything, but we can do a lot; and I contend, without fear of being mistaken, that there is no passion that we cannot overcome when we are fully convinced that it can only serve to make us unhappy.

In our early youth, what leads us astray in this regard is that we are incapable of reflections. We have no experience, and we imagine that we can retrieve the good that we have lost by chasing after it; but experience and knowledge of the human heart teaches us that the more we run after it, the more it escapes us. It is a mirage which disappears when we think we've reached it. Desire is a voluntary thing that requires no persuasion, and which is hardly ever rekindled.

What is your goal when you succumb to the desire that you have for someone? Isn't it to be happy through the pleasure of loving and that of being loved? It would therefore be as ridiculous to refuse oneself this pleasure for fear of an unhappiness to come that perhaps you would experience only after having been extremely happy, (and then there would be compensation, and you ought to think of curing yourself and not of regretting), as for a reasonable person to feel ashamed for not having seized happiness by the hand, but placed it entirely in those of another.

The game of love

The great secret to ensure that love does not make you unhappy is to try never to behave badly or foolishly as regards your lover, to never show an eagerness when your lover cools off, and to always be a degree colder than they are; that will not bring them back, but nothing will. There is nothing to do but to forget somebody who stops loving you; if this person still cares for you, nothing is capable of reviving and restoring the initial ardour of that love except the fear of losing you and of being less loved. I know that it is difficult for tender and sincere souls to adopt this approach. They cannot however be too assiduous in doing so, all the more so since it is much more necessary for them than for others.

Nothing humiliates us more than the lengths to which we go to win back a cold and unfaithful heart. It demeans us in the eyes of the person whom we wish to keep, and in those of potential admirers who might have considered us. But what is much worse, it makes us unhappy and torments us pointlessly. We must thus follow this maxim with an unshakeable courage, and never cast it from our hearts; we must attempt to know the character of the person to whom we are becoming attached, before succumbing to our desire.

Reason must be admitted into our 'council of advisors' - not that reason which condemns all forms of engagement as contrary to happiness, but that which, in agreeing that we cannot be immensely happy without loving, wishes that we love only for our happiness, and that we overcome a desire when it is clear that we would only endure miseries. But when this desire has been most intense, when it has surpassed reason, as happens only too often, we should in no way pride ourselves upon a constancy that would be as ridiculous as it is misplaced. It is then the right moment to put into practice the proverb,

The shortest moments of madness are the best.

Above all, they cause the briefest miseries: for there are moments of wild abandon that would make us exceptionally happy is they lasted a lifetime.

One ought not to be ashamed to have been mistaken. The important thing is to recover, whatever it costs, and above all to avoid the company of the person in question which can only agitate you, and make you forget your resolve: for as regards men, flirtatiousness survives love; they do not want to lose either their conquest or their victory, and by a thousand flirtations, they know how to reignite a fire that is not fully extinguished, and hold you in a state of uncertainty as ridiculous as it is unbearable. One must slice through the heart, break definitively. One must, says Mr de Richelieu*, unstitch the friendship and tear up the love. Lastly, it is for reason to make our happiness: in childhood, our senses alone provide this care; in youth, the heart and the mind begin to blend with them, with this proviso, that the heart decides all; but in maturity, reason must be among the company. It is its purpose to make us feel that we must be happy, whatever it costs.

The passage of time

Each age has its pleasures that are its own. Those of old age are the most difficult to obtain: *gambling* and *study*, if one is still capable of them, *gourmandise, consideration,* these are the pleasures of our later years. All of that is, no doubt, mere consolation. Fortunately, it is in our own hands to bring forward the end of our life, if we are having to wait too long; but for as long as we are resolved to bear it, we must try to make pleasure penetrate by every door open to it just as far as our soul; we have no other reason for living. Let us try, then, to maintain good health, to have no prejudices, to have passions, to make them serve our happiness, to replace our passions by our tastes, to preciously guard our illusions, to be virtuous, to never repent the past, to ward off sad thoughts, and to never permit our hearts to retain a spark of inclination towards someone whose desire is dwindling and who is ceasing to love us.

One day, we must surely leave love behind, if ever we become old, and this day must be when it ceases to make us happy. Lastly, let us consider cultivating a taste for study, this inclination that depends only upon ourselves for our happiness. Let us protect ourselves from ambition, and above all let us be very clear about what we want. Let us decide which route we want to take to spend our lives, and let us try to plant flower seeds as we go.

About the Author – Emilie du Châtelet

To many people outside France the name Emilie du Châtelet will mean very little, unless they happen to have studied 18th century French literature, history, or culture in some depth. Even in France her name, life and work are largely a mystery for most people. This is a great pity, since she was a veritable pioneer in her day, and is a very inspiring example of what a person may accomplish by sheer will, force of personality, and an insatiable curiosity. Her intellectual work was achieved in spite of oppressive social constraints, the lack of predecessors like her to light the way, and an unconducive cultural and intellectual environment.

It is true that Emilie du Châtelet was not born into dire poverty or even social disadvantage, and that she was blessed with a father who believed in the education of girls at a time when most men didn't. She was born into the French nobility and had an arranged marriage at the age of nineteen to a man who was also an aristocrat, though with no great fortune. Nonetheless, the overwhelming majority of women like her were destined to become wives and mothers, lead lives of relative material comfort, and gracefully subside into old age once their children had grown up and married, provided that such women had not already died in childbirth or succumbed to some incurable illness or epidemic.

Emilie du Châtelet did nothing of the sort, and was judged very harshly in polite society – by men and women equally – for flouting the rules of correct behaviour as they applied to women, in both her sentimental and intellectual life. Unlike the majority of women, she lived a very full life in both respects. In fact, it is tempting to wonder whether, until she wrote her reflections on happiness at the age of forty, she was even aware that there were any strict rules of acceptable behaviour, at least as far as she was concerned.

In any case, she had such natural exuberance and such as passionate nature, that they could not have been constrained by the reins of convention and the disapproving mutterings of polite society. Fortunately, she had a very tolerant husband in the Marquis de Chastelet, who turned a blind eye to her successive extra-marital liaisons, and even to her very close intellectual and voluptuous relationship with Voltaire, which lasted well over a decade.

Indeed, Voltaire was as much her soul-mate as her lover, and remained a loyal friend up to her death at the age of forty-three.

It was thanks to her father that she was able to develop her natural talents in mathematics and other disciplines; he arranged for her to have private tuition, including with the celebrated mathematician, Maupertuis. Many years later, while living with Voltaire at the Château de Cirey, she decided to submit a paper to a competition held by the Royal Academy of Sciences.

She wrote this scientific paper – on the nature of fire – in secret and unbeknown to Voltaire, who also sent in an essay on the same subject under his own name. Neither of them won the competition, but both papers were published by the Academy. Emilie du Châtelet thereby became the first woman ever to have her work published by this prestigious scientific institution.

An interesting feature of Emilie du Châtelet's complex personality is that she was in some respects very conventionally feminine, while also being highly rational and cerebral in her intellectual pursuits and disputes with others. It is not widely known that she wrote the first translation from Latin into French of Isaac Newton's great work of mathematics and physics, *Principia.* To accomplish this, she needed to have a full understanding of this masterpiece. Her translation remains the standard French version of reference to this day. In gentle mockery, Voltaire sometimes called her 'Pompom Newton' in reference to her taste for fripperies as well as her enthusiasm for the English mathematician and scientist. After her death, at which Voltaire had been present, he said of her that she had been 'a great man whose only failing was to be a woman'.

Voltaire's posthumous description of her is somewhat ambiguous and open to diverse and opposing interpretations. She was clearly every inch a woman, and places herself firmly in the woman's camp in her private reflections on happiness. She never said or wrote anything suggesting that she would have preferred to renounce her womanhood – though she evidently regretted the social and cultural limitations that it imposed upon her.

However, since the concept of a 'great woman' scarcely existed in her era, she could not seriously be described as such after her death, or receive any public recognition associated with being a great woman. Voltaire's protégé, the philosopher, mathematician, and statesman, Condorcet, would later cite as examples of 'great women', Queen Elizabeth 1 of England and Catherine the Great of Russia, and would call for women to have the right to enter parliament as elected representatives and the right to vote. However, in the late 18th century he was one of very few politicians to entertain the idea that women should be allowed to move beyond the narrow spheres of existence allotted to them at birth, from one generation to another.

Be that as it may, Emilie du Châtelet conducted her own quiet revolution by breaking through the barriers of what it was possible for a woman to achieve in the sciences as well as the arts. Even in the months and weeks preceding the birth of her daughter in 1749, she was arduously working on the completion of her translation of Newton, with her own commentary. Her general health was not good and she had grave misgivings that she might not live much longer - a presentiment that only increased her determination to finish this undertaking.

In this and in other respects, her life was an exception to the rule established by the early 19th century Romantic poet, Lord Byron, according to which, 'Man's love is of his life a thing apart. 'Tis woman's whole existence'. As far as she was concerned, her intellectual passions and pursuits were as much an important part of her life as the affairs of her heart.

Main Events in the Life of Madame du Châtelet

1706   Birth of Gabrielle-Emilie le Tonnelier de Breteuil to Louis Nicolas de Breteuil and his second wife, Gabrielle Anne de Froulay in Paris.

1725   At the age of 19, she marries Florent-Claude, Marquis du Chastelet, whose family are part of the nobility of Lorraine, but with no great fortune.
The marriage is arranged. As a wedding gift, her husband is made governor of Semur-en-Auxois in Burgundy by his father. The couple move there in the autumn.

1726-34   She gives birth to a girl and two boys. They are named Gabrielle-Pauline, born in 1726, Louis Marie Florent, born in 1727 (guillotined during the Terror in 1793), and Victor-Esprit, born in 1734 but destined to die soon afterwards.

1733-1735   She receives tuition in mathematics from Moreau de Maupertius, a member of the Academy of Sciences, and then Alex Clairaut, a mathematical prodigy later celebrated for Clairaut's equation and Clairaut's theorem.

1733   At 27 she meets the writer and philosopher, Voltaire, aged 39, who becomes her lover. He encourages her to study physiques and mathematics, recognizing that she has an aptitude for them. It is also Voltaire that adopts the name of Madame du Châtelet as opposed to Madame du Chastelet. The relationship will last, in one form or another, for fifteen years, i.e. until her death.

1738   She secretly drafts a paper on the nature of fire, which she submits to a competition on this subject held by the Royal Academy of Sciences.

Voltaire also submits a paper. Neither wins a prize but both texts are published by the Academy. Emilie becomes the first woman ever to have a paper published by the Academy (1744).

Her essay on the nature of fire anticipates modern knowledge on infrared radiation and the nature of light.

1740	Her essay entitled Lessons in Physics is published. It is a review of new ideas in science and philosophy, written for her thirteen-year old son, incorporating a synthesis of complex ideas of leading thinkers of the time.

Two other essays, Of the Existence of God and her Analysis of the Philosophy of Leibnitz are also published.

1746	She writes her Reflections on Happiness, (though the precise date is uncertain).
1748	She begins an affair with the poet, Jean-François de Saint-Lambert, and becomes pregnant by him.
1749	She writes a French translation and commentary of Isaac Newton's major work, The Mathematical Principles of Natural Philosophy, from the original work in Latin.

Her commentary presents her own notion of the conservation of energy, which she derives from Newton's principles of mechanics. Her text remains, today, the standard French translation of Newton's Principia Mathematica.

She moves to Lunéville, accompanied by Voltaire.

3rd September, she gives birth to a daughter, Stanislas-Adélaide.
10th September, she dies suddenly of a pulmonary embolism.
Her baby daughter dies 20 months later.

After her death, one of her rings is found to contain a miniature painting of Saint-Lambert, much to the surprise of Voltaire who thought that his own portrait was contained within the ring.

Important events after her death

1756   Her translation of Isaac Newton's Principia Mathematica is published six years after she wrote it. Voltaire said of it, *This translation, which the most learned men of France should have done and that the others should study, a woman has undertaken and completed to the astonishment and glory of her country.*

1779   The first edition of her Discours sur le Bonheur (Essay on Happiness) is published.

1792   Her essay, Doubts on Revealed Religions, is published.

1796   Her Essay on Happiness (or Reflections) is published within 'Opuscules philosophiques et Littéraires' by Imprimerie de Chevet, Paris.

1967   A synthesis of her comments on the Book of Genesis, contained within her critical analysis of the entire Bible, is published in English by Ira O. Wade of Princeton University in his book, Voltaire and Madame du Châtelet: An Essay on Intellectual Activity at Cirey.

2011   A book containing her complete notes on the Bible, edited and annotated by Bertram Eugene Schwarzbach, is published in the original French.

Other works by Madame du Châtelet (not definitive)

-    A French translation of B. Mandeville's The Fable of the Bees in a free adaptation. In the preface, she argues strongly for

women's education on a par with young men, to enable them to excel in the arts and sciences.
- Works on optics, rational linguistics, and the nature of free will.

Notes on the Text

1.   André Le Nôtre (1613 – 1700) served as the main landscape gardener to King Louis XIV, and was responsible for designing the parkland of the Palace of Versailles. Le Nôtre undertook a visit to Italy in 1678, and met Pope Innocent XI in the following year.

2. The story of Renaud and Armide (or Rinaldo and Armida in Italian) forms part of the epic poem *Jerusalem delivered* by the Italian poet Torquato Tasso (1544-1595). During his life, Tasso was described by the Pope as 'the king of poets', and he was later greatly admired by the French philosopher, Jean-Jacques Rousseau. His epic poem provides a very romantic representation of the combat between Christians and Muslims at the end of the First Crusade, and during the siege of Jerusalem.   Rinaldo is a soldier in the First Crusade to bring Christianity to the East. Armida is a Saracen sorceress sent to stop the soldiers from succeeding in their endeavour. Though intending to kill Rinaldo while he is sleeping, she falls in love with him, and he with her. She imprisons him in an enchanted garden. Two of his fellow soldiers find him and rescue him by holding a shield to his face in which he can see his own image, reminding him of who he is and of his duties. Armida is one of many examples in literature of women in love, rejected and abandoned. At the time that Emilie du Châtelet wrote this work on happiness, the story had been dramatized both in theatre and opera productions in France and elsewhere.

3.   Juvenal was a poet born in Ancient Rome at the end of the 1st century AD. He spent his life in Rome and wrote sixteen poetical works, comprising short satirical poems in Latin, contained in one complete volume. He died at the beginning of the 2nd century AD.

4. *Vertu*, or 'virtue' in English, is a concept that has many different definitions, which vary from one religion, culture or epoch to another. It may be described as a philosophical, religious, and/or a political concept. Madame du Châtelet's use of the terms in this essay seems to be greatly inspired by Ancient Greek and Roman thought, and the political philosophy of Montesquieu (1689-1755), the French Enlightenment writer.

He spoke of political *vertu* (the love of the laws and of country). According to him, this love of virtue required that one always gives priority to public interest before personal advantage, and virtue, thus defined, was fundamental to the principle of democracy.

5. The quotation, 'One easily dazzles the eyes of mortals, but one cannot deceive the watchful eye of the gods', is taken from Act I Scene 3 of Voltaire's tragedy in five acts, Sémiramis, which he wrote in 1748. The legend of Sémiramis is thought to be based upon a real historical figure, namely the Assyrian queen, Sammuramat (9th century BC) who was married to Shamshi-Adad V, and was the mother of Adad-Nirari III, as alluded to by the Ancient Greek historian Herodotus.

In Voltaire's play, after the death of her husband Ninos, King of Niniva, Queen Sémiramis becomes regent on behalf of her young son and governs for forty-two years, during which time she founds Babylon, and has built the Gardens of Babylon. She also orders the conquest of the Medea and Armenia, before turning to Egypt and Ethiopia. When she discovers that her son, Ninyas, is plotting against her, she disappears and, according to the legend, is transformed into a dove. It is interesting to note that Madame du Châtelet refers to 'one of our best poets' without mentioning him by name, even though it is he, Voltaire, to whom she refers towards the end of the essay as the person with whom she has had an intimate relationship which lasted many years.

6. Polichinelle is better known as Punch, as in Punch and Judy, the two hand-puppets that used to been seen frequently at puppet shows for children at seaside resorts or, occasionally, on television. The puppet probably first appeared in the Commedia dell'arte in 17th century Italy. He has a long, pointed nose and is cruel, mean, and deceitful, whilst often pretending to be naïve. He always wears a white costume and a black mask, symbolizing life and death. He often carries a plate of macaroni and a wooden spoon, with which he frequently hits Judy and the other puppets.

7. Alexandrine verse refers to poetry or verses in a play written in a specific poetic metre i.e. comprising twelve syllables per line, and usually with a pause, or caesura, between the sixth and seventh syllable. Alexandrine verse, often in rhyming couplets, was very common in French 17th and 18th century poetry, as well as in dramatic works such as those of Corneille and Racine.

8.   Michel Eyquem de Montaigne (1533-1592) was a French philosopher, moralist and essayist of the Renaissance period. He was born at Saint-Michel-de-Montaigne in the Dordogne, and served as the Mayor of Bordeaux.   His Essays influenced and inspired later European authors and philosophers such as Shakespeare, Pascal, Descartes, Nietzsche, Proust, and Heidegger. Evidently, Emilie du Châtelet was quite familiar with his essays, and boldly expresses an alternative perspective with regard to the anticipation of one's own death.

9.   Jean-Baptiste Gresset (1709-1777) was a French poet, playwright, and writer, born in Amiens. He was three years younger than Emilie du Châtelet and would have been living and writing in Paris as one of her contemporaries. He said of Paris, 'On ne vit qu'à Paris et l'on végète ailleurs'. (One lives only in Paris and one vegetates elsewhere).

10.   Marcus Tullius Cicero (106-43BC) was a Roman statesman, orator, and writer. Born in Arpinum to a family belonging to the bourgeoisie, he trained in rhetoric and law. Despite not being a member of the nobility, he garnered sufficient support from allies to obtain a place in the highest court in Ancient Rome, the Consulate. He wrote works in Latin on moral philosophy, including the problems of the search for truth and the quest for happiness, which he described as the goal of all human beings.   His work 'Of supreme good and supreme evil' comprises five books, in which he outlines the replies of contemporary Greek schools of philosophy to the question of how happiness may be attained, and he assesses the merits and demerits of each reply.

11. Madame du Châtelet was well aware of the dangers and pitfalls of gambling. She once lost the enormous sum of 84,000 francs in one evening to card tricksters at the Court of Fontainebleau.   She subsequently devised an ingenious financial scheme, similar to modern day derivatives, by means of which she was able to pay the court gamblers from future earnings.

12. John Wilmot, 2nd Earl of Rochester (1647-1680), referred to in this essay as 'Mylord Rochester', was an English poet and courtier of King Charles II during the Restoration. The contemporary poet, Andrew Marvell, described him as 'the best English satirist', and he was widely admired for his great erudition and wit. His frivolous lifestyle as a libertine and hedonist epitomized the new era of the Restoration and its rejection of the puritanism and authoritarianism of the previous age. His best known work is his Satire against Reason and Mankind.

He died at the very young age of thirty-three. It is usually claimed that his premature death was the result of the venereal diseases, syphilis and gonorrhoea, which were then incurable, combined with alcoholism. However, death from renal failure as a consequence of Bright's disease has also been proffered as an explanation. After his death, it was claimed by a religious associate of his mother, Burnet, who later became Bishop of Salisbury, that on his deathbed he renounced his past libertine lifestyle, underwent a religious conversion, and asked that all his 'profane and lewd writings' be destroyed. As with so many of the smaller (and larger) details of history, the precise truth remains uncertain and obscure.

13. In Ancient Greek mythology, Nestor of Generia was the son of Neleus and Chloris, and he succeeded his father as King of Pylos after the latter, and all Nestor's siblings, were killed by Heracles. As an Argonaut Nestor helped fight the centaurs, and participated in the hunt of the Calydonian Boar. During the Trojan War, as recounted in Homer's Iliad, he fought alongside his sons with the Achaeons, and by this time was already very old. Homer presents him as a man whose advice to younger warriors was greatly respected because of his age and experience.

14. Cardinal de Richelieu (1585-1642) was an ecclesiastic and a statesman. He became the principal minister and advisor to King Louis XIII and, in this primary role, exercised a powerful influence in politics, diplomacy, colonial matters, religious and cultural affairs etc. He played a great role in reinforcing royal power and is regarded as one of the main founders of the modern French state. Many of his pithy statements, or aphorisms, such as those contained within his Memoirs and his Political Testament have frequently been quoted by others owing to their humour, their eloquence, their insightfulness, and their concision.

Examples include: 'Decapitating one's mother is rarely popular with the people, sire. It always looks a touch ungrateful'; 'One should listen a great deal and speak little, to act wisely in the government of a state'; and 'Nothing is as dangerous for the state as those who would govern kingdoms with maxims found in books.' His approach to government is perhaps highlighted in another pithy saying, 'First, use all means to conciliate; failing that, all means to crush'. His approach to unrequited love and diminishing passion seems to have been equally trenchant and decisive, if one is to judge by his assertion that, in such circumstances, one should 'unstitch the friendship and tear up the love'.

A brief note about the editor and translator

Sheila Oakley completed a doctorate on French 18th century history, spanning the period of the Enlightenment and the French Revolution at the European University Institute in Florence in July 2004. Since then she has worked as a writer, editor, and translator. She first discovered Madame du Châtelet's Reflections on Happiness at around the age of forty while strolling through a bookshop, and they left a considerable impression upon her. Though written in the mid -18th century by a very erudite and exceptional woman born into the nobility, these reflections have a universal value, and readers of all ages can appreciate them, and of course concur or disagree with them as they see fit.

To contact the editor/translator, please write to her at:- smoak@outlook.fr

This translation is based upon the 1796 edition of Madame du Châtelet's essay, 'Réflexions sur le bonheur', written in 1746. This first edition was published within 'Opuscules Philosophiques et Littéraires' by the Imprimerie de Chevet in Paris.

The original text in French can be read on the BnF Gallica website:-

gallica.bnf.fr/ark:/12148/bpt6k101933d

Printed in Great Britain
by Amazon